UNCOVERING THE PAST: ANALYZING PRIMARY SOURCES

TRANSCONTINENTAL RAILROADS

NATALIE HYDE

Crabtree Publishing Company
www.crabtreebooks.com

Author: Natalie Hyde

Editor-in-Chief: Lionel Bender

Editors: Simon Adams, Ellen Rodger

Proofreader: Laura Booth, Wendy Scavuzzo

Project coordinator: Petrice Custance

Design and photo research: Ben White

Production: Kim Richardson

Production coordinator and prepress technician: Ken Wright

Print coordinator: Margaret Amy Salter

Consultant: Amie Wright, The New York Public Library

Produced for Crabtree Publishing Company by Bender Richardson White

Photographs and reproductions:
Bridgeman Images: front cover (Promontory Point), Alamy: 13 (Pictorial Press Ltd.), 15 (Everett Collection, Inc.), 18, 27 Left, 35 (Granger Historical Archive), 24 (Stan Zack), 30–31 (ClassicStock), 38–39 (Wikimedia, Andrew Bowden), 39 Bottom (Shutterstock), 40–41 (Trains and Planes), 41 (ton koene); Getty Images: 4–5 (John Dominis), 10–11, 14–15, 31 Mid (Bettmann), 11 (Stock Montage), 14 (Jay Colton/The LIFE Images Collection), 22 (MPI), 24–25 (Otto Herschan); Library and Archives Canada: 27 Rt (Library and Archives Canada); Library of Congress: 1 (LC-DIG-stereo-1s00525), 3 (LC-USZC4-11399), 4, 6 Top Left (Icon) (LC-DIG-stereo-1s00621), 8 Top Left (Icon) (LC-USZC2-3451), 10, 12, 14 Top Left (Icon) (LC-USZC2-3451), 12 (LC-DIG-stereo-2s00632), 16, 18 Top Left (Icon) (LC-DIG-highsm-13375), 20, 22 Top Left (Icon) (LC-DIG-stereo-2s00632), 23 Top (LC-DIG-ppmsca-09855), 24, 26, 28, 30 Top Left (Icon) (LC-DIG-stereo-2s00632), 25 (LC-DIG-stereo-1s00570), 29 (LC-USZ62-133890), 32, 34, 36 Top Left (Icon) (LC-DIG-stereo-1s00618), 36 (LC-USZ62-78251), 37 (LC-DIG-cwpbh-04474); National Archives 6–7 Top (General Records of the United States Government); Shutterstock 38, 40 Top Left (Icon) (Modfos); Topfoto: 6–7 Btm, 8–9, 16–17, 19, 20–21, 21, 23 Btm, 26, 28–29, 31 Btm, 34 (The Granger Collection), 32–33 (Topham Picturepoint).
Map: Stefan Chabluk

Cover photo: The *Driving the Last Spike* painting by Thomas Hill (1829-1881). It depicts the 1881 joining of the Central Pacific (left) and the Union Pacific Railroads on May 10, 1869, at Promontory Point, Utah.
Background: An illustrated page from Crofutt's Trans-Continental Tourist's Guide, 1870.
Title page photo: An 1860s Central Pacific engine runs through the Sierra Nevadas

Library and Archives Canada Cataloguing in Publication

Hyde, Natalie, 1963-, author
Transcontinental railroads / Natalie Hyde.

(Uncovering the past : analyzing primary sources)
Includes bibliographical references and index.
Issued in print and electronic formats.
ISBN 978-0-7787-3941-8 (hardcover).--
ISBN 978-0-7787-3983-8 (softcover).--
ISBN 978-1-4271-2000-7 (HTML)

1. Railroads--North America--History--Juvenile literature. 2. Railroads--Social aspects--Juvenile literature. 3. Railroads--Economic aspects--Juvenile literature. I. Title.

TF148.H93 2017 j385.097 C2017-903633-5
C2017-903634-3

Library of Congress Cataloging-in-Publication Data

CIP available at the Library of Congress

Crabtree Publishing Company
www.crabtreebooks.com 1-800-387-7650

Printed in Canada/082017/EF20170629

Published in Canada
Crabtree Publishing
616 Welland Ave.
St. Catharines, ON
L2M 5V6

Published in the United States
Crabtree Publishing
PMB 59051
350 Fifth Avenue, 59th Floor
New York, NY 10118

Published in the United Kingdom
Crabtree Publishing
Maritime House
Basin Road North, Hove
BN41 1WR

Published in Australia
Crabtree Publishing
3 Charles Street
Coburg North
VIC, 3058

UNCOVERING THE PAST

INTRODUCTION

THE PAST COMES ALIVE

*"**History** is the landmark by which we are directed into the true course of life."*

Marcus Garvey (1887–1940) Jamaican National Hero and black nationalist leader

The **society** we live in now can be traced back to the thousands of decisions, both big and small, made in the past. Some were great ideas, others were tragic mistakes, but each one contributed to the industries, **cultures,** and governments we have today. By studying the past, we can better understand the present. We can see how our thoughts, ideas, and **prejudices** shape our world.

Big ideas are always a risk. Linking the east and west coasts in North America was seen as a way to unite a country. Both the United States and Canada saw railroads as the means to do this. The west would become **accessible** to people from the east, as well as European **immigrants** who wanted to settle there. Goods and resources from the west coast, mountains, and prairies could flow east. Railroads would make long-distance travel for passengers quicker and more comfortable. With not enough workers to get the job done, foreign laborers from Ireland and China were brought in. Although they helped build the railroads, the Chinese laborers could not easily become **citizens.** It started a wave of immigration that would be impossible to reverse. Railroad development brought each nation together, but it also pushed European settlers into the territories of western **Indigenous peoples.**

This book looks at the construction of the transcontinental railroads in North America in the mid- to late 1800s, and the impact they had on the settlement and growth of the United States and Canada. Railroads were first developed in England, where they are called railways, and some early North American companies used the title "railway."

▲ Engineer Theodore Judah's first official map of the eastward-reaching Central Pacific Railroad. It was filed in 1862, the day before U.S. President Abraham Lincoln signed the Pacific Railroad Bill into law.

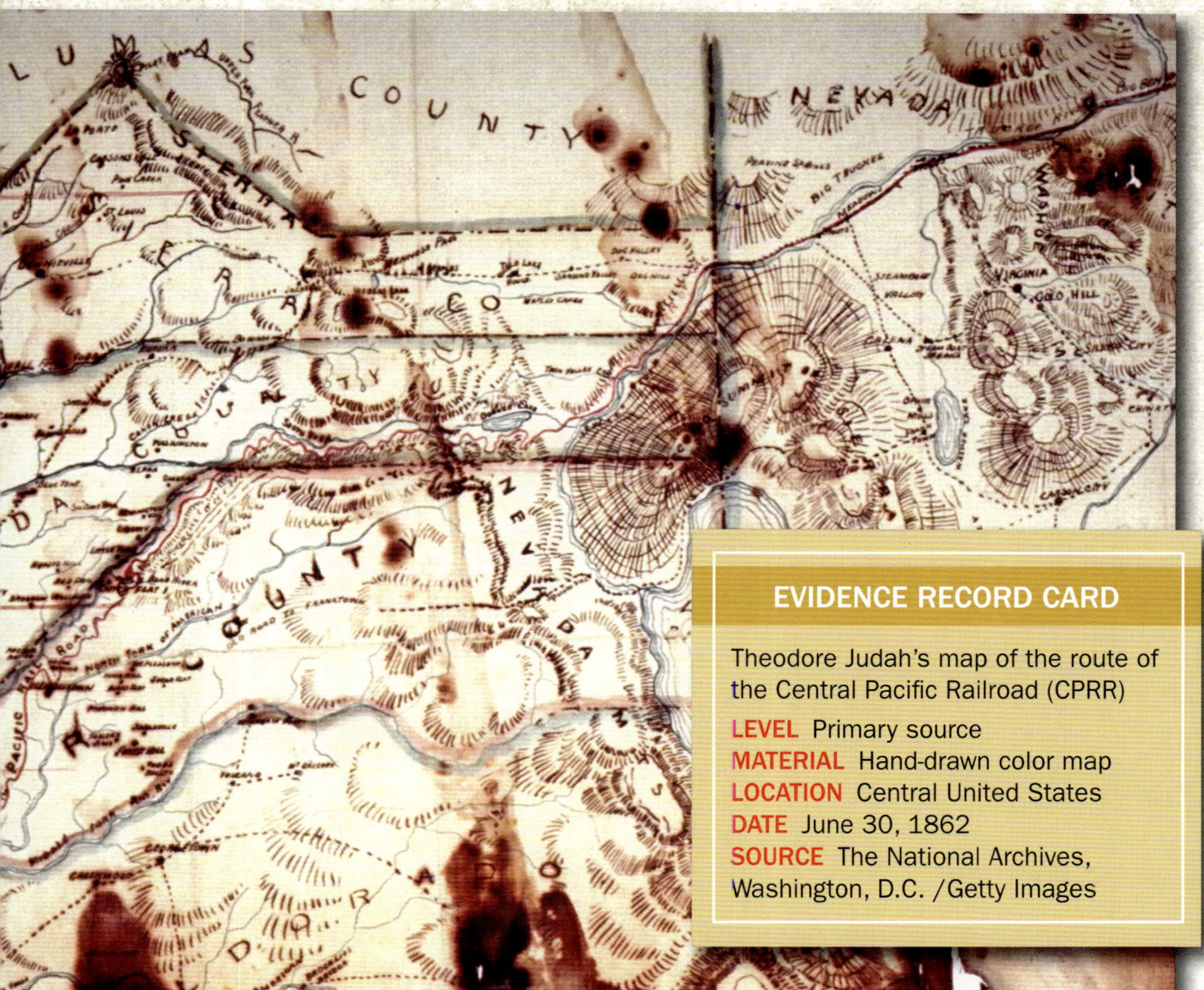

EVIDENCE RECORD CARD

Theodore Judah's map of the route of the Central Pacific Railroad (CPRR)

LEVEL Primary source
MATERIAL Hand-drawn color map
LOCATION Central United States
DATE June 30, 1862
SOURCE The National Archives, Washington, D.C. /Getty Images

DEFINITIONS

Historians use special words to talk about time:
Decade: A period of 10 years.
Century: A period of 100 years.
Millennium: A period of 1,000 years.
Generation: A group of people who were born at about the same time.
Era: A period of time dominated by an important characteristic, event, or person.
Age: A long period of time dominated by an important event such as the Industrial Age. Railroads were part of the Industrial Revolution.

INTRODUCTION

WHERE TO LOOK FOR EVIDENCE

We can learn about our past in many different ways. We can listen to oral stories told by older generations. We can read written accounts from individuals, **journalists,** or governments. We can interview people who lived through past events, or examine old paintings, photographs, and sculptures. We can read books on a subject to gather more information or gain a new **perspective**. Each piece of information adds details and insights to help us understand the reasons an event happened or why a person acted the way they did.

To begin a search to learn about our past, we can look in museums, libraries, or private collections. We can also ask a historian. A historian is someone who researches, studies, and writes about the past. He or she is often an expert in one area, event, or time period. Jack Simmons (1915–2000) was an English historian who specialized in railroad history. Stephen Ambrose (1936–2002) was another historian who focused on American history and wrote about the building of the Pacific Railroad. This book uses their research.

Depending on the time and place when an event happened, it can be easy or hard to find information. For example, very old events may have happened before cameras were invented, so there may not be any photographs. Wartime could mean all

Congress of the United States,
At the Session
BEGUN AND HELD AT THE CITY OF WASHINGTON
in the District of Columbia
AN ACT
Be It Enacted by the Senate and House of Representatives of the United States of America in Congress assembled

> *"T.D. Judah & Co., civil engineers & railroad contractors, are prepared to execute and furnish surveys, plans and estimates, to contract for and to build and equip railroads in the state of California, on the most favorable terms."*
>
> Advertisement in *Placer Herald* from Auburn, California, July 21, 1860

documents in a museum were burned or bombed. There might be a lot of information on a celebrity because of media attention.

Because the building of the transcontinental railroads in both Canada and the United States were **sanctioned** by the governments, there is much evidence. Official records, reports, laws, and acts were based on the idea of connecting regions of the countries by rail. Photography was new but was still able to capture many important moments during the construction. Because much of the land to be crossed was mostly unexplored, maps were drawn to help the railroads find the best routes.

◀ **The Pacific Railroad Act, signed by President Lincoln on July 1, 1862, allowed the construction of a rail and telegraph line from the Missouri River in the east to the Pacific Ocean in the west.**

◀ **This cartoon of May 1869 celebrated the completion of the transcontinental railroad in the United States.**

PERSPECTIVES

Take a close look at the illustration of the locomotives. How does the illustrator portray Native Americans? Do you think he shows a **bias**, or unfair opinion? What clues in the picture back up your answer?

TYPES OF EVIDENCE

"The very ink with which all history is written is merely fluid prejudice."

U.S. author Mark Twain, 1897

Evidence about an event, a person, or a place is called **source material.** Sources are anything that has been left behind by the past. They are the building blocks of our understanding. Source material can be created by companies, artists, or ordinary people. It can be the result of someone's work or hobby, or it can be created by accident. Sometimes source material is well known. Important **artifacts** are often on display in museums for everyone to see. Libraries allow everyone to borrow historic materials and study them. Ruins or monuments are out in the open and can be visited by everyone.

Sometimes source material is **controversial.** It might remain hidden because its existence could be dangerous to the people who own it. During World War II (1939–1945), Germans who had papers or photographs of Jewish people might be accused of helping them and be punished themselves by the Nazi government. At other times, source material is **preserved** by accident. Old newspapers might be used to pack china in an attic. Letters or reports might be lost during a move and found later in an unexpected spot. The cargos of ancient ships might be sealed in a shipwreck deep in the ocean. Paintings might be hidden in a cave for protection.

Source material for the transcontinental railroads is usually easy to find. Government and company reports, maps, and records are available for the public to read. They are kept in museums or libraries. Photographs, maps, engineering drawings, newspaper articles, and magazine articles can be viewed online as well as in actual archives.

▼ Chinese laborers of the Central Pacific Railroad (CPRR) helped build snow sheds. These wooden structures kept snow off the tracks by letting avalanches slide right over top.

ANALYZE THIS

Reread the quotation by Mark Twain at the top of page 8. What do you think he means? In what ways was source material about the building of the transcontinental railroads written with prejudice?

HISTORICAL SOURCES

PRIMARY SOURCES

There are two types of source materials: primary and secondary. **Primary sources** are firsthand accounts or direct evidence of an event. They are often created at the time the event happened. Primary sources can be visual, auditory, written, or artifacts. Visual sources are things you can see such as photographs, paintings, posters, illustrations, and maps. Auditory sources are things you can hear such as music, speeches, and interviews. Artifacts are objects that were used or part of an event or a person's belongings.

Some primary written sources include:

- Diaries and journals: stories written down about daily life
- Newspapers: Printed reports on daily events in a certain area
- Blogs: Journals posted on the Internet
- Reports: Documents written for businesses or governments to show progress
- Advertisements: A flyer or space in a newspaper to offer items for sale or rent
- Lyrics: The words of a song
- Letters: **Correspondence** on paper between two people
- Social media: Updates on social sites online

▼ The railroads opened up the west to families wanting to settle there. In the United States, the Homestead Act of 1862 gave 160 acres (65 hectares) of land for farming to Americans and foreigners wanting to immigrate. These settlers are plowing their land in Custer County, Nebraska.

"Tell the President that the grading of the first forty miles main line Union Pacific Railway was finished yesterday at three oclock. This has been accomplished in forty five working days."

Samuel Hallett, railroad developer, in a telegram to the U.S. government in 1863

Primary written source material for the building of the transcontinental railroads across Canada and the United States includes new maps drawn by engineers looking for a suitable way across water or through mountain ranges. **Invoices** for materials to build the railroads were created, and reports were written for the governments. Newspapers covered everything from the laying of the first rails to the hammering of the last spike. The men who worked on the railroads wrote letters back to their families, and musicians wrote lyrics to songs capturing the thoughts and feelings of life along the rail line.

▼ This advertisement from 1876 offers homes on "Railroad Land" along the line. This would give **homesteaders** access to supplies, mail, and transportation from rural areas.

A Farm of Your Own
The Best Remedy for Hard Times!
FREE HOMESTEADS
AND THE
Best and Cheapest Railroad Land
Are on the Line of the
Union Pacific Railroad,
IN
NEBRASKA.
SECURE A HOME NOW.
Full information sent FREE to all parts of the world. Address
O. F. DAVIS
Land Com'r U. P. R. R., Omaha, Neb.

ANALYZE THIS

The railroads plowed through land inhabited by Indigenous peoples. Why would the railroad companies be so eager for families to settle along the rail lines?

VISUAL EVIDENCE

Old paintings can give us an idea of how things looked before cameras were invented. Sculptures and statues give us an idea of how our ancestors viewed the world. Historic maps let us learn about how much of the world had been explored and how much was settled. Photographs capture a moment in time.

Primary visual sources include:

- Posters: Printed images with or without words
- Paintings: Images created on canvas
- Photographs: Images made with a camera
- Maps: Diagrams of a region or area
- Movies/videos: Moving images recorded by a camera
- Billboards: Large outdoor boards showing advertisements
- Flyers/brochures: Small pamphlets with information about services or products
- Tapestries: Images woven with fibers
- Drawings: Sketches and etchings

The building of the transcontinental railroads produced a lot of visual **evidence**. In the United States, each company hired its own photographer to follow the progress along the route. They had to bring bulky and heavy equipment across difficult **terrain**. Some even had a wagon as a mobile **darkroom**. During the building of the Canadian Pacific Railway, the official photographer Frank Haynes used a stereo camera. It produces two images that are almost identical. They are then viewed in a stereoscope machine to make the image look 3-D.

▼ **Stereoscopic** images of a steam locomotive on the U.S. trancontinental railroad in Nevada in about 1869.

CENTRAL PACIFIC RAILROAD

UTAH.

349 Scene near Deeth. Mount Halleck in distance.

During survey work to find the best routes across the prairies and through the mountains, delicate and expensive camera equipment wasn't practical. Instead, artists were hired to sketch or make watercolor prints. These images give us a great sense of the wild landscape before the railroads. Posters, maps, political cartoons, and illustrations of the construction and the finished railroad brought the project to life.

AUDITORY SOURCES

Songs captured the feeling of the start of this new era with music such as the Union Pacific's "Grand March." Workers on the railroads also created their own songs reflecting their experiences. "The CPR Line" and "900 Miles" are two traditional songs about building the railroads. At first, the songs were learned by repetition and practice, but they were later written down and recorded.

▶ **Advertisements promoted the speed and comfort of the new rail line with "sleeping cars," "eating houses," and a trip to San Francisco of "less than four days."**

EVIDENCE RECORD CARD

Poster advertising passage on the new U.S. transcontinental railroad

LEVEL Primary source
MATERIAL Printed poster
CREATED FOR Union Pacific Railroad
DATE May 10, 1869
SOURCE Pictorial Press–Alamy

HISTORICAL SOURCES

SECONDARY SOURCES

Sometimes source materials are created long after an event and are not based on firsthand experience. These are called **secondary sources**. Secondary sources can present new perspectives on an event. They can also explain how an event affected ordinary people, governments, and society at the time and afterward.

How can you tell whether something is a primary or secondary source? Read the document carefully while asking yourself these questions: Does the author or creator get their information from someone else's work (instead of personal experience)? Is the creator **interpreting** events or drawing conclusions (instead of giving facts)? Is the date of the work long after the date of the event (instead of matching closely with it)? If the answer is "yes," then the material is likely a secondary source.

Secondary sources include:

- Novels, movies, poems, songs: Stories that might be based on actual events
- Paintings, engravings, and cartoons: Visual representations of what may have happened
- Textbooks: Books used in schools to give information on a topic
- Magazines: Publications with written articles

Novels such as *Blood and Iron: Building the Railway* (I Am Canada) by Paul Yee (2010) relate what life may have been like for a young boy working on the building of the railroad. It describes the **primitive** and violent life in "hell on wheels" towns.

PERSPECTIVES

In studying the movie still from *Union Pacific*, what impression do you get about the conditions for people working on the railroad? What details in the image support your answer? Do you think this is an accurate representation of what it was like?

▲ In his travel book *Roughing It*, from 1872, Mark Twain tells of life in the Wild West with the coming of the railroads.

"We know the Red Beards here do not like us. But we are doing a good job building the railway, aren't we? That makes me sad, to think that no matter how hard we work, the Red Beards still dislike us."

from *Blood and Iron: Building the Railway, Lee Heen-gwong, British Columbia, 1882* (I am Canada) by Paul Yee

▶ *Canadian Pacific* was filmed in 1948–49 in the Canadian Rockies along the Canadian Pacific Railway's transcontinental route.

EVIDENCE RECORD CARD

Movie still from *Union Pacific*
LEVEL Secondary source
MATERIAL Photograph
CREATED FOR Cecil B. DeMille and Paramount Pictures
DATE 1939
SOURCE Getty Images

▲ The 1939 movie *Union Pacific* used so many trains to recreate the U.S. transcontinental railroad that the film company had to get a railroad operating license.

INTERPRETATION

"If history can do anything it is to remind us of those complications that undermine our certainties, and to show us that all our judgments are merely relative to time and circumstance."

Herbert Butterfield, British professor of history, in 1931

Historians know that source material is of varying importance and value. Sometimes the creator of documents or images may favor one idea over another. The source that is created will reflect their viewpoint. This is called bias. Bias can change what material is created or how it is **portrayed**. To help them, historians often use the Bias Rule.

- Every piece of material must be looked at **critically.**
- The creator's point of view must be considered.
- Each piece should be compared with other sources to determine the level of bias.

Many of those who built the transcontinental railroads were recent immigrants or Chinese laborers. Some people believed that they were a strong work force. Other people felt the Chinese laborers were there to "take away" jobs from white workers. How the Chinese were portrayed in political cartoons, paintings, or in documents depended on the bias of the creator. There was also a strong bias concerning the Indigenous peoples living on the plains. Many people of white European backgrounds called them "savages" and believed they were primitive and **uncivilized**.

It is important to understand and identify bias when looking at source material to be able to see through it to the truth. Both primary and secondary sources can show bias, as many transcontinental railroad examples in this book clearly show.

▶ The Chinese, in their conical, bamboo hats, labored from sunrise to sunset, six days a week on the railroads. They set an example with their hard work and reliability. Irish railroad laborers felt threatened by the Chinese workers who worked longer hours for lower pay.

EVIDENCE RECORD CARD

Image of men working on the last mile of Central Pacific Railroad.
LEVEL Primary source
MATERIAL Wood engraving
LOCATION One mile (1.6 km) from Promontory, Utah
DATE about 1869
SOURCE The Granger Collection/ Topfoto

PERSPECTIVES

Study the image closely. What information do you get about the ease or difficulty of laying the tracks? There are European and Chinese workers pictured here—the hats help you tell the difference. What does the image tell you about how the work was divided?

ANALYZING

As well as looking for bias, historians use the Time and Place Rule to judge the quality of the source material. The rule states that the closer in time and place the creation of the source was to an event in the past, the more accurate it is likely to be. Historians also try to learn about the context, or setting, in which evidence was created. Understanding what was going on at the time helps us to explain why people would have certain beliefs and prejudices. It can help establish why certain **slogans** or images became popular.

In the United States, California was **annexed** after the Mexican–American War of 1846–1848. The idea of a transcontinental railroad to connect the different territories of the nation was gaining popularity. In Canada, the building of the transcontinental railroad came at a time that the nation was expanding from the east coast to the west coast.

Historians also note that railroad construction began after the gold rushes in California (1848–1855) and in the Klondike in Canada (1886–1899). In both cases, many Chinese laborers had come to work in the gold fields. Once the rushes were over, the laborers were out of work. Thousands were hired to build the railroads. In the United States, once the availability of Chinese laborers from California was gone, the railroads hired laborers directly from China. Soldiers returning from the U.S. Civil War (1861–1865) in particular saw this as a threat to their own abilities to find work. All these changes were in the context of building the transcontinental railroads.

▼ On the Union Pacific Railroad, immigrants were treated like second-class citizens. Trains had separate "immigrant cars" and railroad stations had separate waiting rooms for them.

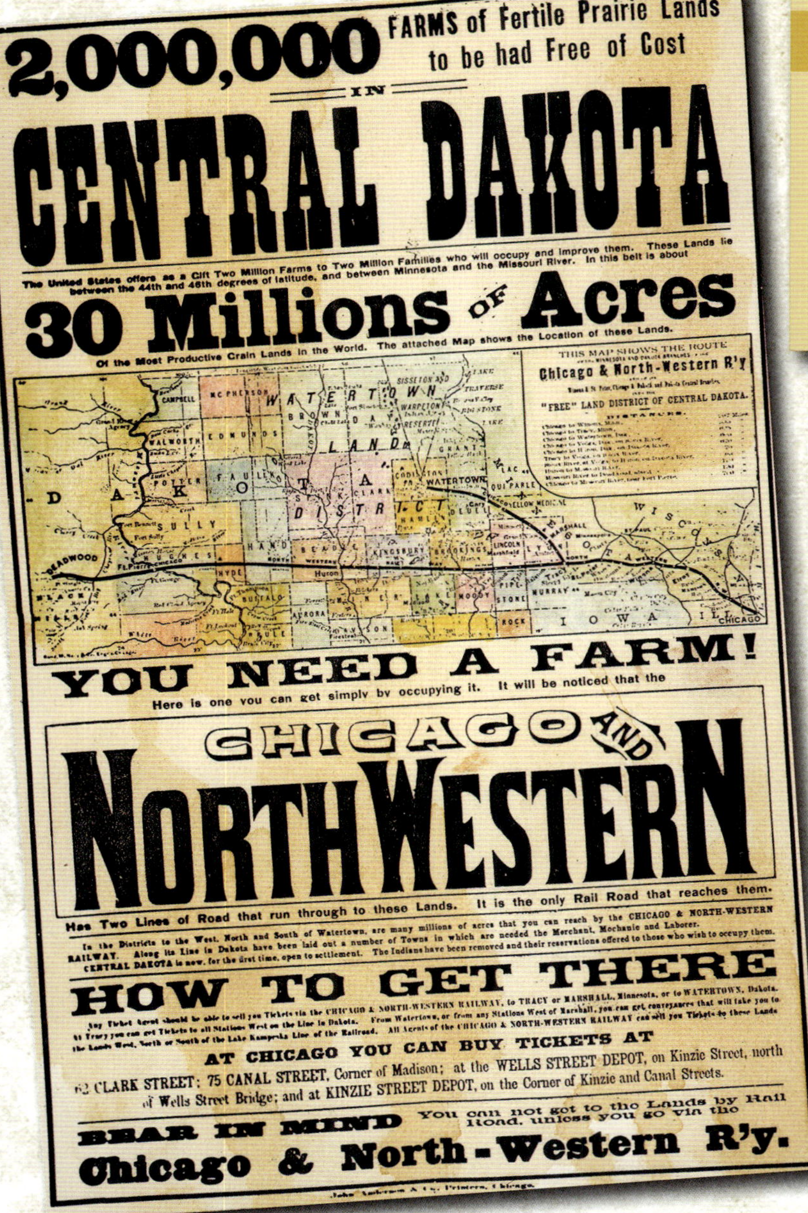

EVIDENCE RECORD CARD

Railroad company poster
LEVEL Primary source
MATERIAL Advertising poster
LOCATION Chicago
DATE about 1870
SOURCE The Granger Collection/Topfoto

◀ The land offered to citizens had been given to the railroad companies by the government. Previously, that land had been gained from Native Americans through treaties in which they were taken advantage of through low payments for large acreage and loopholes removing many of their rights.

PERSPECTIVES

Who created this advertisement for free farms? Did they have something to gain from giving away land? Do you think the information encouraging people to move is reliable? Or is there bias? How do you know?

"Dear Sir: The snow cover to be built next season will require more nails & spikes of certain large sizes than can be found in this market unless we order them expressly. Please tell me lengths & kinds wanted & about how many per mile."

Excerpt from letter of March 10, 1868, by Mark Hopkins, constructor of the Central Pacific Railroad

BUILDING THE RAILROADS

*"The one moral, the one remedy for every evil, social, political, financial, and industrial, the one immediate **vital** need of the entire Republic, is the Pacific Railroad."*

Rocky Mountain News, 1866

Before planes jetted people around the world, and cars sped along highways, trains were a fast and dependable way for people and **freight** to move. In North America, the first railroad tracks were built on the east coast to transport goods such as coal and granite from their sources to cities and piers.

In the United States in the early 1800s, the Louisiana Purchase, the Mexican–American War, and the Gadsden Purchase all expanded the country's borders. The government saw the building of a railroad linking east and west as a way to open the west for settlers and allow goods and services to flow across the country. By the 1860s, Americans believed that they were **destined** to settle the west. They called this Manifest Destiny and it became the reason for building railroads and removing Native Americans from their land.

In Canada during the same time frame, most transportation was either by wagons on roads or by barges on waterways. Roads were rough and waterways were frozen for months each year. With a bit of maintenance, railroads were good year round. Canada was also growing. In 1871, British Columbia agreed to join the **Confederation** with the promise of a transcontinental railway to be built within 10 years. Construction began in 1881 and was finished just four years later.

▶ **The Union Pacific and Central Pacific Railroads meet at Promontory Point, Utah, in the United States.**

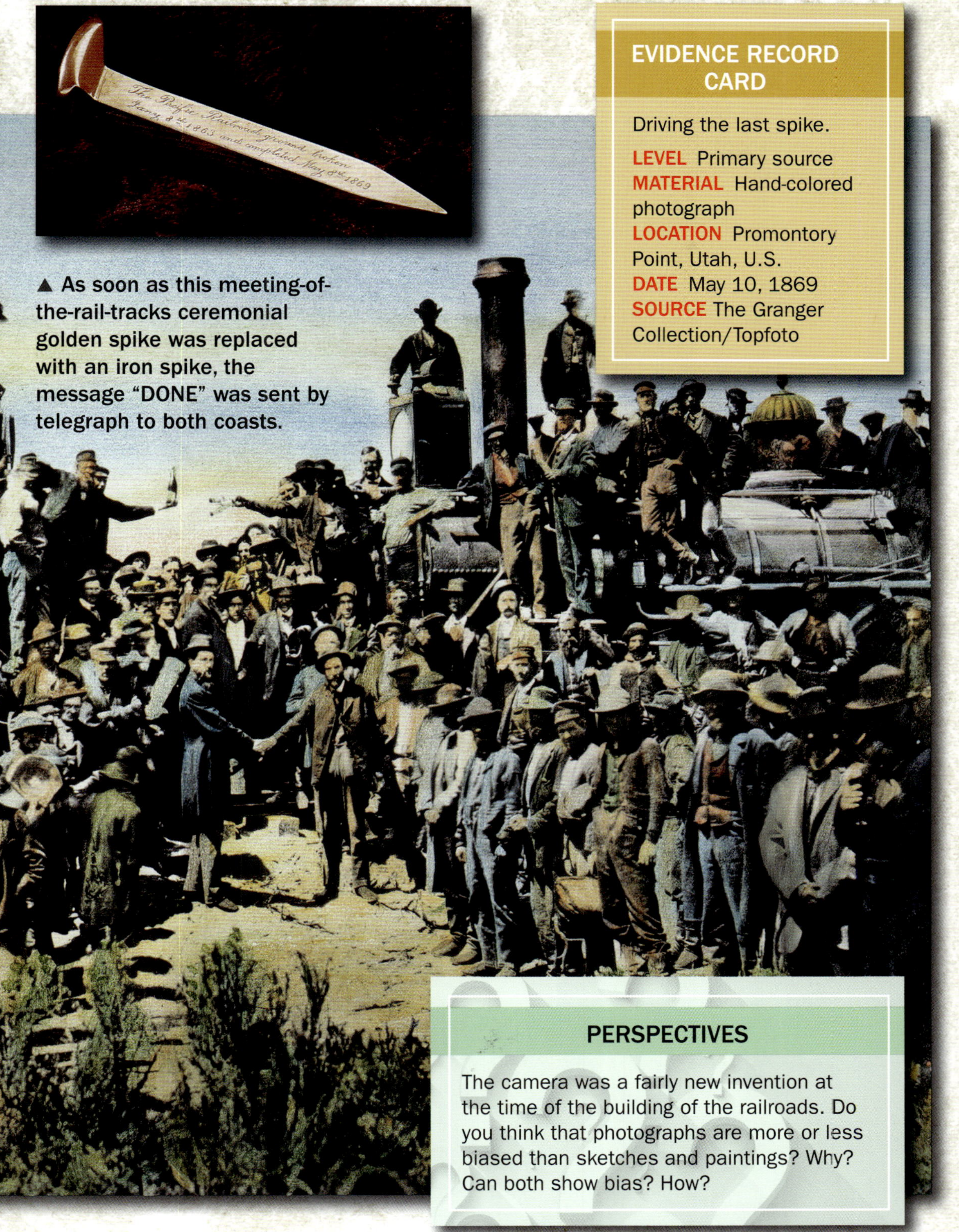

▲ As soon as this meeting-of-the-rail-tracks ceremonial golden spike was replaced with an iron spike, the message "DONE" was sent by telegraph to both coasts.

EVIDENCE RECORD CARD

Driving the last spike.

LEVEL Primary source
MATERIAL Hand-colored photograph
LOCATION Promontory Point, Utah, U.S.
DATE May 10, 1869
SOURCE The Granger Collection/Topfoto

PERSPECTIVES

The camera was a fairly new invention at the time of the building of the railroads. Do you think that photographs are more or less biased than sketches and paintings? Why? Can both show bias? How?

GOVERNMENT SUPPORT

Just before the building of the transcontinental railroad in the United States, people had been traveling by train up and down the east coast. But those wanting to head west had to make the difficult and dangerous journey over mountains, plains, rivers, and deserts. They risked being attacked by Native Americans who were protecting their lands. Others chose to travel by sea and took the six-month journey around Cape Horn at the tip of South America, or risked **yellow fever** by crossing the Isthmus of Panama and then traveling by ship up the west coast.

A better way was needed both for people and for freight. **Surveyors** investigated five different routes. President Abraham Lincoln signed the Pacific Railroad Act in 1862, which gave land grants and loans to private railroad companies for the construction.

In Canada, the private firm Canadian Pacific Railway (CPR) was also helped out by the government. It was given $25 million in cash, land grants, rights-of-way, and even a ban on competing rail lines for 20 years. Some questioned the high cost of a route through the Canadian

PERSPECTIVES

Look closely at the image of the **pioneer** family. How many supplies do you think you could pack in this wagon? What would you have to leave behind? Looking at the landscape, what do you think one of the most important supplies might be?

▼ Before the railroads, travel across the prairies of North America was slow and dangerous. Settlers died of diseases such as cholera from polluted water sources.

◀ In this painting, Manifest Destiny is leading the European settlers from east to west across the United States.

▼ This flyer from about 1850 advertises the slow sea route from New York to San Francisco.

Merchants' Express Line of Clipper Ships

FOR

SAN FRANCISCO!

NONE BUT A 1 FAST SAILING CLIPPERS LOADED IN THIS LINE.

THE EXTREME CLIPPER SHIP

OCEAN EXPRESS

WATSON, COMMANDER,

AT PIER 9, EAST RIVER.

This splendid vessel is one of the fastest Clippers afloat, and a great favorite with all shippers. Her commander, Capt. WATSON, was formerly master of the celebrated Clipper "FLYING DRAGON," which made the passage in **97 days**, and of the ship POLYNESIA, which made the passage in **103 days**.

She comes to the berth one third loaded, and has very large engagements.

RANDOLPH M. COOLEY,

118 WATER ST., cor. Wall, Tontine Building.

Agents in San Francisco, De Witt, Kittle & Co.

Shield of northern Ontario. By March 1885, the CPR was not finished and in debt. Still it was used to send troops to Saskatchewan to help end the North-West Rebellion, where **Métis** and other Indigenous peoples had resisted further settlement of their lands. Because of this success, the government agreed to reorganize CPR's debt and give them another loan to help finish the project.

With the completion of both transcontinental railroads, travel across North America became faster, safer, and cheaper. Before the railroads, travel from coast to coast could cost about $1,000. After they were built, a ticket cost about $150, making the journey easily accessible.

"It will populate the vast territory and be the great highway of the nations; their merchants will cross it to trade with us. But there is another aspect, which we view it as a blessing, and in connection with which we esteem of it still greater importance. It will preserve the union of these States."

Excerpt from address by Rev. Dr. Vinton at Trinity Church. (*Harper's Weekly*, May 29, 1869)

RAILROAD COMPANIES

In the United States, the building of the transcontinental railroad was set up as a competition between two companies. In Sacramento, California, the Central Pacific Railroad Company started on the west coast and built a way through the Sierra Nevada mountain range. Theodore Judah was a civil engineer who had helped build the first railroad in California. He had arranged for four wealthy merchants—Leland Stanford, Collis Huntington, Mark Hopkins, and Charles Crocker, known as the "Big Four"—to **finance** that railroad. When Judah proposed building a transcontinental railroad, they agreed to back it, too.

In the east, the Union Pacific Railroad built westward from the Missouri River near the Iowa–Nebraska border. The two lines of track met somewhere in the middle. To encourage a faster result, the companies were promised 6,400 acres (2,590 hectares) of land and $48,000 in **government bonds** for every mile (1.6 km) of track built.

In Canada, British Columbia insisted that a railway be built from the east to the Pacific coast as a condition for joining the Confederation in 1871. After some controversy, Canadian Pacific Railway was given the contract and a deadline to complete the rail line in 10 years.

One of the biggest **obstacles** was finding a route through the Rocky Mountains. Instead of a northern route, CPR decided to use the more direct Kicking Horse Pass. This famous pass had one section with a dangerous, steep drop. They called it the Big Hill. That section caused several runaway trains. The route

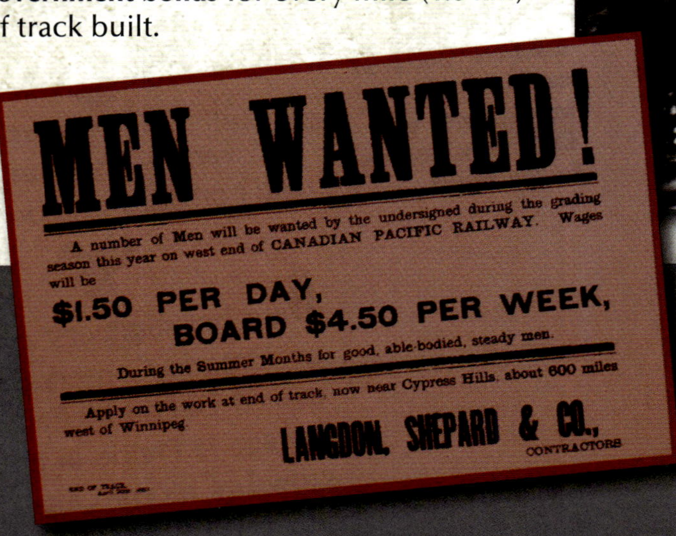

◀ "Navvies," a nickname for navigational engineers, were mainly Irish immigrants. At $1.00 to $2.50 per day, they made almost double the wage of Chinese railroad workers.

also crossed the lands of the Blackfoot tribe. Eventually, Chief Crowfoot granted them permission. He was given a lifetime pass to ride the CPR. Canada's transcontinental railway was finished six years early, on November 7, 1885.

▲ Snowplows attached to the front of locomotives worked to keep tracks clear through the winter.

ANALYZE THIS

What could be the benefit of having two companies compete for land and cash to build from opposite ends of a country to meet somewhere in the middle? What could the benefit be for one company to start at one end and go straight through to the other? If you were in charge of a project like this, which method of working would you choose? Why?

◀ Railroad companies first used wood to build trestles and bridges because it was cheap and plentiful. The wooden beams were later replaced with metal.

"Our quarters were at the east end of Donner Pass, but still in the narrow part. About the second or third day of a storm the wind would be a gale... and would plough up the new-fallen snow to heap it in huge drifts beyond the east end of the pass. About thirty feet from our windows was a large warehouse; this was often hidden completely by the furious torrent of almost solid snow that swept through the gorge."

John R. Gilliss, Central Pacific Railroad civil engineer

CHINESE AND IRISH LABOR

The first years of construction for the two American railroad companies were uneven. The Union Pacific started to lay track in Omaha, Nebraska, in 1865. They had no problem finding labor with so many Civil War veterans, mostly Irishmen, out of work. They faced a lot of **resistance** from Native Americans, though, as they laid track across the homeland of the Apache, Cheyenne, and Arapaho. Railroad workers were armed against frequent raids by Native Americans who were angry that they were being forced off their lands.

The Central Pacific on the west coast had a slow start through the mountains. It also had trouble finding labor. Irish laborers had to be shipped out west and many left the railroad to work in gold and silver mines. Eventually, the railroad decided to hire the Chinese workers who no longer worked in the gold mines.

▼ Chinese workers were called "coolies." This was a slur for a low-paid, immigrant laborer. Most came from southern China, trying to escape the poverty in their homeland after a civil war.

"The Great Central Iowa Route now open between Omaha and Chicago via Des Moines & Rock Island. The quickest time ever made between Missouri River and Chicago is via this Great Central Route–Over 100 miles shorter than via St. Joe and no change of cars. This line is well stocked with elegant new cars and Palace Sleeping Coaches for all through trains."

Salt Lake Daily Telegraph and *Commercial Advertiser*, September 7, 1869

The transcontinental railroad in Canada started with the formation of the Canadian Pacific Railway Company in 1881. The first year of construction was a disaster with only 131 miles (211 km) of track laid. A new manager, W. C. Van Horne, took over and the next year—despite floods in the spring—workers laid 418 miles (673 km) of the main line. After that, work progressed quickly.

All along the rail lines, temporary communities sprang up. Merchants were the first to arrive and offered goods and services to the railroad workers. Others came to set up dental offices, gambling dens, saloons, and law offices. There were few **permanent** buildings—most services were provided in tents. As the line moved on, the town was abandoned and set up farther down the route, often leaving little behind. These were called tent towns.

▼ As well as being paid less than white workers, Chinese workers in Canada were given the hardest and most dangerous work, clearing the railbed or setting explosives.

◀ Railroad directors traveled in private railcars. Seated at the main table are officials of the Union Pacific Railroad.

ANALYZE THIS

Compared to railroad workers, railroad financiers and officials became wealthy. Do you think this was fair? Why should they have received greater rewards? Were the workers exploited or were they lucky to be given work? How would you feel having to do hard work for six days a week?

THE STORY UNCOVERED

IMPACT ON INDIGENOUS PEOPLES

As the transcontinental railroads grew, Indigenous peoples watched as their land, ways of life, and future were stripped from them with every rail laid.

Across the United States, Native Americans fought back with raiding parties. They tried to slow or stop construction by attacking surveyors and workers. They stole livestock and supplies. They removed laid rails and derailed locomotives. Still the railroad grew. Land that tribes had hunted and lived on was divided by a steel line. All along it, towns grew and the trains brought more and more settlers west to take over and farm the land.

In Canada, the land between the eastern colonies and British Columbia was called Rupert's Land. It was home to several Indigenous peoples such as the Cree. The conflict between them and the Canadian Pacific Railroad was similar.

The U.S. and Canadian governments dealt with the different tribes by creating more than 350 treaties. They broke the treaties almost immediately when the land was needed for the railroads. The treaties were written with loopholes that allowed the railroads to buy even more land and limit the movements of the Indigenous peoples and Native

▶ Construction of the transcontinental railroads forced Native Americans, Indigenous peoples—and buffalo—off their traditional lands in the west.

"I represent the whole Sioux nation, and they will be bound by what I say. I am no Spotted Tail, to say one thing one day and be bought for a pin the next. Look at me, I am poor and naked, but I am the Chief of the nation. We do not want riches, but we want to train our children right. Riches would do us no good. We could not take them with us to the other world. We do not want riches, we want peace and love."

Chief Red Cloud's speech to White Brethren at Cooper Institute, from *The New York Times*, June 17, 1870

Americans. Most were relocated to **reservations.** The belief in America's Manifest Destiny—that the European settlement to the west was bound to happen and that they deserved to have that land—made it easy for the railroads, merchants, and settlers to justify breaking the treaties.

The transcontinental railroads also affected one of the main sources of food for many Indigenous peoples—the buffalo. The rail lines cut through buffalo **migration** routes and separated herds. Also, the trees that were cut down for railway ties, buildings in towns, and bridges, meant less habitat for all types of wild game. Kept on reservations, the Indigenous peoples' ways of life and culture were damaged forever.

PERSPECTIVES

Study how Indigenous peoples were portrayed in this colored wood engraving of 1867. Do you think this image was created by a white or an Indigenous artist? Why do you think so? How might it be different if it were created by the opposite artist?

▲ As the railroads headed west, millions of buffalo were killed accidently or for meat, bonemeal, and sport. Railroad companies, settlers, and travelers had little concern for the Indigenous peoples that depended on buffalo.

THE STORY UNCOVERED

FINISHING THE RAILROADS

The completion of each transcontinental railroad was marked with the hammering of a "last spike" into the rail lines. In the United States, the two competing railroads met at Promontory Point, Utah, on May 10, 1869. Telegraphers announced the news that the railroad was complete at 12:57 P.M. People celebrated around the country. The trip from New York to California that used to take six months could now be made in two weeks. The wild **frontier** was quickly settled by European immigrants and the traditional ways of life of Native Americans came to an end.

▼ Along the U.S. transcontinental railroad, there were stations every 8 miles (12.9 km). This meant steam locomotives could load up more water and coal to continue.

"The new highway thus opened to man will not only develop the resources, extend the commerce, increase the power, exalt the dignity and perpetuate the unity of our Republic, but in its broader relations, as the segment of a world-embracing circle, directly connecting the nations of Europe with those of Asia, will materially facilitate the enlightened and advancing civilization of our age."

Congratulatory Dispatch, Special Committee of U.S. transcontinental railroad, May 10, 1869

In Canada, the final spike was driven in on November 7, 1885, at Craigellachie in British Columbia. A silver spike had been made for the event, but because of bad weather, it didn't arrive in time.

Not everyone was celebrating, though. Indigenous peoples' lives were destroyed. Chinese immigrants who had left their homeland to find work, now faced unemployment and **discrimination.** The immigrants who stayed found work as servants, opened businesses, or went to work on other rail lines. In Canada, the Chinese Immigration Act of 1885 imposed an expensive head tax to discourage them from staying.

Many Chinese workers in the United States stayed on to help with the expansion of the transcontinental railroad into new lines. After that, they looked for jobs in factories or on farms. The Chinese Exclusion Act of 1882 ended Chinese immigration. It was the first law that prevented an ethnic group from immigrating to the U.S., and it added to the fear that the Chinese were a threat.

CENTRAL PACIFIC RAILROAD.

NO. 1, TIME CARD NO. 1.

To take effect Monday June 6th, 1864, at 5 A. M.

TRAINS EASTWARD.						TRAINS WESTWARD.		
Frt and Pass No 3	Frt and Pass No 2	Pass & Mail No 1.		STATIONS.		Frt and Pass No 1	Pass & Mail No 2.	Frt and Pass No 3.
5 P M leave	1 P M leave	6.15 A M, L		Sacramento.		8.45 A M arr	12 M arr.	6.40 P M ar.
5.50 / 5.55 mt frt	2.15	3.55	18	Junction.	18	3	11.20	5.55 / 5.50 mt. Ft
6.09	2.38	7.05	22	Rocklin.	4	7.40	11.07	5.37
6.22	2.55	7.15 meet F.	25	Pino.	3	7.15 mt pass	10.56	5.25
6.40	3.30 P M arr	7.30 A M arr	31	Newcastle.	6	3.45 A M, L	10.30 A M, L	5 P M, L

Trains No. 2 and 3 east, and 1 and 3 west, daily, except Sunday. Trains No. 1 east and 2 west, daily.

LELAND STANFORD, President.

◀ **The first transcontinental railroad timetables like the one pictured here could fit on a small card. As more trains and rail lines were added, timetables grew to folded, stapled booklets.**

ANALYZE THIS

The transcontinental railroads were built to unite the United States and to unite Canada. This did not always mean each population was united. In what ways did the railroads divide people?

▶ **Transcontinental railroad dining cars, like this one in 1877, had excellent food and service.**

EVIDENCE REVISITED

"May God continue the unity of our country as this railroad unites the two great oceans of the world"

Inscription on the commemorative last spike, U.S. transcontinental railroad

Some believed the transcontinental railroads brought **prosperity** and opportunity, with farming and mining as well as jobs in the towns all along the lines. Others thought the railroads brought poverty and vices such as gambling and drunkenness.

After the railway was built in Canada, the CPR transported farm workers from the eastern provinces to the prairies in the fall. They charged low fares because they knew they would make their money moving the harvest as freight. They also hoped workers would want to stay and settle in the west and buy land owned by the railroad. Within 10 years of the railroad's completion, it was also already shipping about $50 million worth of freight from coast to coast every year. Clearly for businesses, the transcontinental railroad boosted the economy.

In a U.S. Census report from Joseph Kennedy in 1862, he describes all the changes that had taken place:

". . . More than fifty millions of acres of land were brought into ***cultivation*** *. . . More than 22,000 miles of railroad were completed . . . to indicate on the map of our country the lines of telegraph would be to represent the web of the spider over its entire surface . . ."*

For others in the United States, opening up the west created a line of poverty. Newspaper articles from 1869 claimed the railroad brought a "shifting about." Every month, the residents of towns in the west would change as workers moved on down the line and settlers tried to move in and make a living. Temporary "hell on wheels" towns developed.

▲ For payday on the railroads, the paymasters' car pulled up; the cashiers opened the doors; and they passed out money to the workers.

EVIDENCE RECORD CARD

Payday on the line.
LEVEL Primary source
MATERIAL Black and white photograph
CREATOR Union Pacific Railroad
LOCATION Blue Creek Station, Utah
DATE 1864–1865
SOURCE Topfoto

PERSPECTIVES

Look closely at this image. Do the workers look rested, well-fed, and well-dressed? Or do they look tired, thin, and shabbily dressed? Were there women and men? What does it tell you about the working conditions on the railroads?

STRIKES AND PROTESTS

Immigrant workers are often seen in two lights: Some people believe they are the solution to labor problems. Others see them as taking jobs away from citizens, bringing crime, and never leaving again. Source material from the building of transcontinental railroads shows that these two views existed for Chinese workers.

The Chinese were given some of the hardest and most dangerous jobs. They worked up to 14 hours a day and risked their lives by placing explosives to blast through mountains. While they worked on the railroads, the Chinese workers' dependability, work ethic, and

▼ This cartoon from about 1880 shows that unions representing workers at the time were anti-Chinese. Because the Chinese worked for less pay, they were seen as competition and a threat to non-Chinese workers looking for jobs.

"...a large number of these men are scattered throughout the province without any visible means of support...They systematically evade taxation...and there are no means available of compelling them to contribute their fair share to the Provincial Revenue."

Transcript from the legislature of British Columbia, 1884

FRANK LESLIE'S ILLUSTRATED NEWSPAPER

No. 1,141—Vol. XLIV.] NEW YORK, AUGUST 11, 1877. [Price, 10 Cents.

ILLINOIS.—THE RAILROAD STRIKES AND LABOR RIOTS—COLONEL AGRAMONTE'S CAVALRY CHARGING ON THE MOB, AT THE HALSTEAD STREET VIADUCT, IN CHICAGO, JULY 26TH.—See Page 365.

▲ **After the U.S. transcontinental railroad was finished, the huge amounts of money lent to build it caused a financial crisis across the United States. Thousands of people blocked the rail lines to prevent trains from moving. The cavalry was called in to break up the crowds.**

skill were admired and respected. But once work on the railroads was done, attitudes changed. The Central Pacific released Chinese workers in April 1869 with the completion of the railroad at Promontory, Utah. When the workers returned to the west in search of new work, they met with resistance. The government passed the Chinese Exclusion Act that stopped future Chinese immigration and denied **naturalization** for those already in the United States.

Things were just as bad for the Chinese railroad workers in Canada. The head tax payment each Chinese immigrant had to make to come to Canada kept increasing. In 1923, the government banned immigrants from China altogether. Many of the Chinese laborers that remained in Canada and the United States opted to open their own businesses rather than try to find employment. The ban on Chinese immigrants wasn't lifted until 1943 in the U.S. and 1947 in Canada.

ANALYZE THIS

Why do you think public opinion of Chinese laborers changed so much from the time they worked on the railroads to after the railroads were finished?

"I wish to call to your minds that the early completion of this railroad we have built has been in large measure due to that poor, despised class of laborers called the Chinese, to the fidelity and industry they have shown."

CPRR Director Edwin Crocker

DIFFERENT VIEWS

INDIGENOUS PEOPLES RISE UP

The relationship between the railroads and the Indigenous peoples was complicated. Many businessmen and government officials saw them as a "**menace**" and something to be overcome. They made treaties with them, then broke the treaties in their desire to get the land they needed. This, of course, caused many conflicts. After an attack by the Sioux on the Bozeman Trail, commander of the U.S. Army, William Sherman, said of the attackers: *"We must act with vindictive earnestness against the Sioux even to their extermination, men, women, children."*

There was only one tribe that had a relationship with the U.S. government: The Pawnee were bitter enemies of the Sioux and allowed the government on their lands. The railroad offered free passage on the work trains, which they gladly accepted. Under Major Frank North, a uniformed **battalion** of 800 Pawnee men patrolled the railroad to protect crews and livestock from Sioux raiders. *"I have never seen more obedient or better behaved troops. They have done most excellent service."*

In Canada and the U.S., bison, or buffalo, was the primary food source of the Indigenous peoples of the plains. The buffalo habitat was taken over by settler farms and they were hunted almost to extinction. Métis farmers and hunters feared the loss of the buffalo, their land, and feared a government that did not listen. Led by Louis Riel, the Métis rebelled in 1869 and again in 1885. The second rebellion was called the North-West Rebellion.

"The more we can kill this year the less will have to be killed the next year, for the more I see of these Indians the more convinced I am that they all have to be killed or be maintained as a species of paupers."

Gen. William T. Sherman on the Plains Indians

▲ Artist Thomas Nast created this illustration for *Harpers Weekly* magazine in 1869. It shows the conflict between the railroad and the Indigenous peoples.

PERSPECTIVES

What clues in this image tell you how the Indigenous chiefs approached their talks with the U.S. government about their situation? After more than 10 years of the transcontinental railroad being in operation, what do you think were each party's objectives for the high-powered talks?

The Métis were outnumbered by government troops and this uprising ended quickly. The result of the rebellion for the Métis and their Cree and Assiniboine allies was not better terms but proof that the Canadian government could quickly and cheaply move troops by rail to put down a conflict. For Louis Riel, the end of the rebellion resulted in his capture, trial, and hanging.

▼ Native American chiefs meet with U.S. government officials in 1887 to discuss the impact of the transcontinental railroad.

EVIDENCE RECORD CARD

Sioux and Arapahoe delegation meet with U.S. government officials
LEVEL Primary source
MATERIAL Black-and-white photograph
LOCATION Omaha
DATE 1877
SOURCE Library of Congress

HISTORY REPEATED

"Discount air fares, a car in every parking space, and the interstate highway system have made every place accessible–and every place alike."

Ronald Steel, American historian and author

The transcontinental railroads of the United States and Canada were built to unite each country's east and west coasts. They would allow for people and goods to move quickly and safely from one side of the country to the other.

As reliable as train travel was and is, it has limitations. Technology has also changed and trains are no longer the vital link they once were. Within 30 years of the transcontinental railroads' construction, a new form of private transportation was gaining ground over the public transportation of train travel. Automobiles gave travelers more freedom as they linked not just major cities along relatively straight lines, but into remote areas as well. Automobiles required a new network of roads and highways. Like the transcontinental railroads, the Interstate Highway System in the United States, and the Trans-Canada Highway system in Canada, crisscross both countries. Cars, buses, and trucks now move people and freight as fast or faster than trains. Roads also branch off the highways and go in all directions.

Major highways are enormous government-funded building projects. They have altered landscapes and the ways people live. Highways make it easy for people to live farther away from the cities where they work. Just as cities and "railway towns" built up around stops on the transcontinental railways, they also began to spread out, or "sprawl" around highways. These sprawling housing areas, called *suburbs*, are now common around North American cities.

▶ The Trans-Canada Highway is the longest highway in the world running from the Pacific coast to Atlantic coast of Canada. Parts of the highway follow close to the transcontinental railway tracks.

ANALYZE THIS

In what ways are transcontinental or intercontinental railroads better than air or road routes for moving people and freight? Think of the weight of cargo, weather, and traffic concerns.

MODERN EXAMPLES

RAILROADS TODAY

What role do North America's transcontinental railroads play today?

In the United States, only parts of the original route are still in use. Some sections were abandoned as newer, more direct routes, were built. The country still has one of the largest and most complex freight rail systems in the world. The railroad claims that shipping goods this way helps cut down on clogged roads, highway accidents, and **greenhouse gases**. Forty percent of goods are carried by rail in the United States, especially heavy freight moving long distances.

With the opening of the St. Lawrence Seaway in Ontario and Quebec, rail lost its claim to being the cheapest and fastest way to move freight in eastern Canada. More than 100,231 ton (100,00 metric tonnes) of cargo moves along the marine route each year. In the 1990s, CP Rail sold or abandoned its rail lines east of Montreal, cutting off links to New Brunswick. While it is still possible to travel coast to coast by rail, it is not seamless. Travelers have to change trains several times while riding on lines owned by different companies. Yet Canada's freight railroads still move about $280 billion worth of goods each

▲ At a railyard in Vancouver, Canada, trains with intermodal freight containers and tankers wait to be moved.

ANALYZE THIS

What are some of the benefits of moving passengers and cargo by rail today? What are some of the drawbacks?

"Simply put, we believe that the NEC must be improved to accommodate more trains, operating at faster speeds with significantly reduced trip-times, and with improved service reliability in order to meet the long-term mobility and economic development needs of the region."

Joe Boardman, Amtrak president and CEO, about improvements to the railroad system of the Northeast Corridor region (NEC)

year, including food, cars, fuel, and lumber. Much of the transportation is **intermodal**—cargo stays in one container that is moved onto ships, trains, and trucks. Companies use whichever transportation method is cheapest and fastest in different parts of the country or world.

Railroads in North America are also working to improve safety, speed, and comfort, and lessen their effects on the environment. Passenger rail transportation has been increasing as people find **commuting** by train to be fast and efficient. Amtrak in the United States is planning to move to high-speed rail by 2021. These new trains will lower their use of energy, becoming "greener."

▼ A glass-topped railcar on the Rocky Mountaineer train in British Columbia allows tourists to have a good view of the scenery.

TIMELINE

1840

1860

1862

1864

1866

1841 First settlers move to the west of the United States on what will become the Oregon Trail

1850 In the United States, California becomes the 30th state in the Union

1853 The first cross-border railroad in North America begins running between Montreal, Canada, and Portland, Maine

July 1860 Civil engineer Theodore Judah finds Donner Pass—a route suitable for trains through the Sierra Nevada mountains

Nov. 1860 T.D. Judah and four other investors form the Central Pacific Railroad Company

July 1, 1862 President Abraham Lincoln signs the Pacific Railway Bill in the United States

Jan. 8, 1863 Engineer Leland Stanford shovels the first load of dirt in Sacramento, California, for the start of the Central Pacific Line

Oct. 26, 1863 Central Pacific Railroad spikes its first rails

Nov. 2, 1863 Theodore Judah dies of an illness

Dec. 2, 1863 Union Pacific Railroad breaks ground in Omaha, Nebraska

Nov. 29, 1864 The Sand Creek Massacre of 150 unarmed Cheyenne and Arapaho in land grab for U.S. settlers and railroads

Jan. 7, 1865 Cheyenne, Arapaho, and Sioux raiders retaliate for Sand Creek Massacre

Apr 9, 1865 The American Civil War ends

July 10, 1865 The first rails of the Union Pacific lines are spiked in Omaha

Summer 1865 Central Pacific begins hand-drilling tunnels through the Sierra Nevada Mountains

By Dec. 1865 More than 6,000 Chinese men are working for Central Pacific Railroad

July 1866 Union Pacific has laid 100 miles (161 km) of track

Nov. 1866 North Platte, Nebraska, is the first of many "hell on wheels" towns

June 25, 1867 Chinese workers in Sierra Nevada strike for better wages and shorter hours; the strike fails and they go back to work for the same wage

July 1, 1867 Confederation unites four provinces into Canada

Aug. 28, 1867 Central Pacific workers blast through rock of Summit Tunnel, the last major obstacle of the Sierra Nevada

Apr. 28, 1869 Union Pacific workers set a record by laying 10 miles (16 km) of track in a single day

1871 British Columbia joins Confederation with condition of having a transcontinental railroad built within 10 years

Nov. 7, 1885 Construction of Canadian Transcontinental Railway complete

1870

1880

1885

Nov. 6, 1868 American Indian leader, Red Cloud signs the Powcer River Treaty, which guarantees the Sioux their hunting grounds

May 10, 1869 The Union Pacific and Central Pacific rail lines are joined at Promontory Point, Utah

1878 Construction of Canadian Transcontinental Railway begins; Port Moody, British Columbia, is decided as the end station

Transcontinental railroads in the United States (1869) and Canada (1885)

BIBLIOGRAPHY

QUOTATIONS

p.4: Marcus Garvey quote: Jacques-Garvey, Amy (ed.). Philosophy and Opinions of Marcus Garvey: Africa for the Africans. The Journal of Pan African Studies, 2009, p. 4.
p.8: Twain, Mark. Following the Equator: A Journey around the World. Hartford, Connecticut, 1897, Chapter 69.
p.16: Butterfield, Herbert. The Whig Interpretation of History. W. W. Norton and Company, 1965.
p.20: The Rocky Mountain News, 1866.
p.25: Utah Historical Quarterly, Winter 1969, Vol. 37, No. 1, pp. 41–57.
p.32: Inscription on the gold Last Spike, Stanford Family Collection, Stanford University Museum.
p.34: Saxton, Alexander. "The Army of Canton in the High Sierra." Pacific Historical Review, May 1966, pp. 141–152.
p.35: Journals of the Legislative Assembly of the Province of British Columbia, Vol. 13, p. 38.
p.36: McDonough, James Lee. William Tecumseh Sherman: In the Service of My Country: A Life. W. W. Norton & Company, 2016.
p.38: Ronald Steel quote: https://www.brainyquote.com/quotes/quotes/r/ronaldstee114007.html
p.40: Boardman, Joe: THE AMTRAK Vision for the Northeast Corridor—2012 Update Report. https://www.amtrak.com/ccurl/453/325/Amtrak-Vision-for-the-Northeast-Corridor.pdf, p. 2.

EXCERPTS

p.6 Placer Herald from Auburn, California, July 21, 1860. http://discussion.cprr.net/2007/09/judah-ad.html
p.10: Telegram, Nov. 19, 1863, to Hon. John P. Usher. http://memory.loc.gov/cgi-bin/ampage?collId=mal&fileName=mal1/195/1959700/malpage.db&recNum=0
p.14: Yee, Paul. Blood and Iron (I Am Canada). Scholastic Canada, 2010.
p.19: Letter to M. Arthur Brown, Sacramento, March 10, 1868. http://www.sacramentohistory.org/admin/photo/321_814.pdf
p.25: Abstract of a Paper read before the American Society of Engineers, Jan. 5, 1870, http://cprr.org/Museum/Tunnels.html
p.26: Salt Lake Daily Telegraph and Commercial Advertiser, September 7, 1869. http://cprr.org/Museum/Ephemera/Salt_Lake_Tel_Ads_1869.html
p.28: Red Cloud speech. The New York Times, June 17, 1870. https://static01.nyt.com/images/blogs/learning/pdf/2015/

TO FIND OUT MORE

Non-fiction:

Chan, Arlene. *Righting Canada's Wrongs: The Chinese Head Tax and Anti-Chinese Immigration Policies in the Twentieth Century.* Toronto, Lorimer, 2014.

Floca, Brian. *Locomotive.* New York, Atheneum, 2013.

Perritano, John. *The Transcontinental Railroad.* New York, Children's Press, 2010.

Thompson, Linda. *Building the Transcontinental Railroad.* (History of America) Florida, Rourke Educational Media, 2014.

Fiction:

Durbin, William. *Until the Last Spike: The Journal of Sean Sullivan*. New York, Scholastic, 2013.

Yee, Paul. I Am Canada: *Blood and Iron.* Markham, Scholastic Canada, 2010.

Yin. *Coolies.* London, Puffin Books, 2003.

INTERNET GUIDELINES

Finding good source material on the Internet can sometimes be a challenge. When analyzing how reliable the information is, consider these points:

- Who is the author of the page? Is it an expert in the field or a person who experienced the event?
- Is the site well known and up to date? A page that has not been updated for several years probably has out-of-date information.
- Can you verify the facts with another site? Always double-check information.
- Have you checked all possible sites? Don't just look on the first page a search engine provides. Remember to try government sites and research papers.
- Have you recorded website addresses and names? Keep this data so you can backtrack and verify the information you want to use.

WEBSITES

Travel through time with this newsletter-style trip aboard the Canadian Pacific Railway:
http://sssicamous.ca/wp-content/uploads/2014/01/Canadian-Pacific-Rail-Childrens-Information-Pack-History.pdf

Maps and FAQs for kids interested in the transcontinental railroad, from American Historama:
http://www.american-historama.org/1866-1881-reconstruction-era/transcontinental-railroad.htm

An interactive map from PBS lets you see the seven-year race across the United States to complete the track:
http://www.pbs.org/wgbh/americanexperience/search/?q=railroad

MULTIMEDIA

Learn about the Chinese workers and their role in building the transcontinental railroad in the United States in this PBS video:
http://bit.ly/2n1071i

GLOSSARY

accessible Easily reached

annexed Added to a territory

artifacts Objects made by human beings

battalion A large group of troops

bias Prejudice in favor of or against one thing, person, or group.

citizens People who have full rights to live in a country

commuting Traveling between work and home

Confederation The joining of the colonies to form the country of Canada

controversial Brings about disagreements

correspondence Writing letters back and forth

critically Involving careful judgement about the good and bad parts of something

cultivation Farming land

cultures The ideas, customs, and behaviors of a group of peoples

darkroom A room for developing photographs

destined Meant to be

discrimination Treating people badly based on differences

evidence A body of facts or information to show whether something is true

finance To put up the money to invest in a project

freight Goods or cargo transported by trucks, trains, ships, or planes

frontier The wilderness beyone settled land

government bonds Monetary loans from people to the government that are paid back at an agreed time with an agreed rate of interest

greenhouse gases Gases released into the air from the burning of fossil fuels, in particular coal, oil, and natural gas.

history The record of a particular time or event that has happened in the past

homesteaders People who acquire land and build a house on it to live in; they sometimes also farm the land they live on

immigrant Someone who enters a country or region from somewhere else to live and/or work permanently

Indigenous peoples Original inhabitants of a region or country: in the United States often called American Indians or Native Americans; in Canada often called First Nations, Aboriginal, or Native peoples

intermodal Changing from one mode, or method, of transport to another

interpreting Explaining the meaning of

invoices Statements of the monies due for goods or services

journalists People who write for newspapers or magazines

menace A threat or danger

Métis People in Canada with both Indigenous and European heritage

migration Animals moving from one area to another each year or season

naturalization Becoming a citizen of a country

obstacles Things that block the way

permanent Made to last

perspective Point of view

pioneers People who were among the first to settle a new country or area

portrayed Shown or represented

prejudices Harmful opinions not based on facts

preserved Saved in its original condition

primary sources Firsthand memories, accounts, documents, or artifacts from the past that serve as historical records about what happened at a particular time or event

primitive Considered uncivilized, simple, or sometimes savage

prosperity Good fortune, wealth, and success

reservations Land set aside, often by treaty, for use by First Nation or Native American peoples

resistance Refusal to submit to an authority or accept something

saloons Bars

sanctioned Allowed, approved, agreed upon

secondary sources A historian's or an artist's interpretations of primary sources

slogans Short phrases used in advertising

society A group of people forming a single community with its own distinctive culture and institutions

source material Original document or other piece of evidence

stereoscopic Usomg two lenses and two slightly different pictures or photos that come together to show a three-dimensional (3-D) image

surveyors People who figure out the size, shape, and boundaries of pieces of land

telegraph A form of communication involving electrical signals flowing along wires

terrain Piece of land

transcripts Written version of something spoken or recorded

treaties Agreements between the government and Indigenous peoples to provide them with small areas of land (reserves) in exchange for taking over their traditional territories

uncivilized Not well governed or organized

vital Extremely important

yellow fever A serious viral infection that is spread by certain types of mosquitoes

INDEX